LATTER-DAY CHRISTIANITY

BASIC ISSUES

10

Edited by
Robert L. Millet
Noel B. Reynolds

Contributors
Larry E. Dahl
Robert L. Millet
Daniel C. Peterson
Stephen E. Robinson
Brent L. Top
John W. Welch

FOUNDATION FOR ANCIENT RESEARCH AND MORMON STUDIES
and RELIGIOUS STUDIES CENTER,
Brigham Young University,
Provo, Utah

Cover: This representation of the First Vision of the Prophet
Joseph Smith was painted by Floyd Breinholt. It is used by
permission of Claudia Breinholt and of Alan and Karen Ashton,
who own the painting.

Library of Congress Cataloging-in-Publication Data
Latter-Day Christianity: 10 basic issues / edited by Robert L.
Millet, Noel B. Reynolds; contributors, Larry E. Dahl . . . [et al.].
    p. cm.
Includes bibliographical references.
ISBN 0-934893-32-2 (alk. paper)
1. Church of Jesus Christ of Latter-Day Saints—Doctrines.
2. Mormon Church—Doctrines. I. Millet, Robert L. II. Reynolds,
Noel B. III. Dahl, Larry E.
BX8635.2.L38 1998
230' .9332—dc21   98–41029
                              CIP
05 04 03 02 01 00 99 98   6 5 4 3 2 1

Foundation for Ancient Research and Mormon Studies
P. O. Box 7113, University Station
Provo, Utah 84602

The Foundation for Ancient Research and Mormon Studies is a
nonprofit educational foundation, affiliated with Brigham Young
University, that fosters research on the Book of Mormon and other
ancient scripture. For more information, call 1-800-327-6715.

CONTENTS

Detail from *Christ and the Rich Young Ruler,* by Heinrich Hofmann.

PREFACE

With the rapid and visible growth of the Church of Jesus Christ of Latter-day Saints, it is inevitable that doctrinal differences will arise between Latter-day Saints and people of other faiths. Members of the LDS Church profess to be Christians, to be followers of Jesus Christ and recipients of his redeeming grace. They are not, however, associated with either Catholicism or Protestantism. Mormons believe that God called Joseph Smith in 1820 to restore saving truths and divine powers that had been lost to the world after the deaths of Jesus and his early apostles. They believe that he was commissioned to establish an organization—the Church of Jesus Christ of Latter-day Saints—that is a restoration of the original Church of Jesus Christ. They believe that it possesses the fulness of the gospel of Jesus Christ and is led today by divinely called modern apostles and prophets.

In spreading this message of the restoration to the world, Latter-day Saints do not wish to offend people of other faiths. There are clearly people of every Christian denomination who have devoted their lives to following the Lord, to serving others, and to spreading the message of redemption in Christ to the world. And there are people outside Christianity who live admirable lives devoted to the truths they understand. To Christian and non-Christian alike, the invitation of the restored Church of Christ is to come and see—see if the restored gospel does not have value for your lives, through the truths and powers restored by the Savior of mankind.

Latter-day Saints know that not all will accept this invitation. Yet they do not believe that doctrinal differences should motivate men and women to be less than Christian or civil in their interactions with persons of other faiths. There are so many problems in society—moral and ethical issues on which people of goodwill wholeheartedly agree—that it seems counterproductive to dissipate our strength or dilute our effectiveness when we could so easily join hands in stemming the tide of indecency and immorality.

Further, there is a pressing need in today's world for people of various religious denominations to better understand one another. Nothing good comes from misrepresenting another's beliefs. We hope that addressing a few of the questions most frequently asked about LDS beliefs and practices will contribute to understanding between Latter-day Saints and their friends of other faiths. The ten specific questions considered here get at the heart of the LDS faith and way of life.

That persons outside our own faith may disagree with our position on this or that matter is understandable; that our position should be misstated or misrepresented is, however, not helpful to anyone.

The contributors to this booklet are all members of the faculty of Brigham Young University: Larry E. Dahl is professor of Church History and Doctrine; Robert L. Millet is dean of Religious Education and professor of Ancient Scripture; Daniel C. Peterson is associate professor of Asian and Near Eastern Languages; Noel B. Reynolds is associate academic vice president and professor of Political Science; Stephen E. Robinson is professor of Ancient Scripture; Brent L. Top is associate dean of Religious Education and professor of Church History and Doctrine; and John W. Welch is Robert K. Thomas Professor of Law.

We gratefully acknowledge others who helped with the preparation of this booklet: colleagues who read and critiqued our work; editors at FARMS who provided numerous suggestions and carried out the production of the booklet, including Donald L. Brugger, Lesa Shearer, Wendy C. Thompson, and Melvin J. Thorne; Scott Knudsen, who designed the booklet; Alan and Karen Ashton, who allowed us to use their painting by Floyd Breinholt for our cover; and Claudia Breinholt, who generously gave permission for the use of her late husband's painting.

While this is not an official publication of the Church of Jesus Christ of Latter-day Saints or Brigham Young University, the contributors have sought in their expressions to be in harmony with scripture and the teachings of modern church leaders. Each of the contributors has worked for many years in the educational system of the LDS Church and has taught and written a great deal on the topics discussed in this work. While much more could be said on these topics, we hope that this brief treatment will be sufficient to respond appropriately to questions that continue to arise.

Only when people are unafraid of truth will they find it. Therefore, we invite all to follow the admonition of Paul: "Prove all things; hold fast that which is good" (1 Thessalonians 5:21).

Robert L. Millet
Noel B. Reynolds

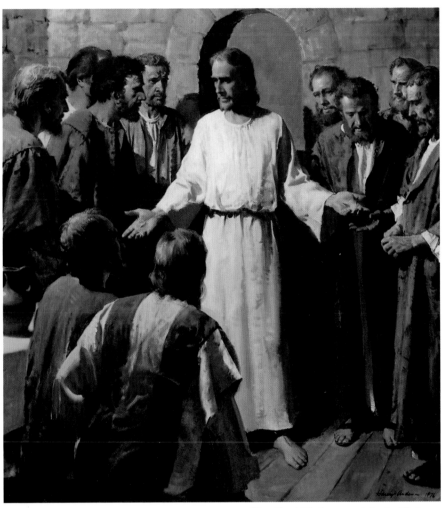

We talk of Christ, we rejoice in Christ, we preach of Christ, we prophesy of Christ, and we write according to our prophecies, that our children may know to what source they may look for a remission of their sins. 2 NEPHI 25:26 [Painting by Harry Anderson, Behold My Hands and Feet]

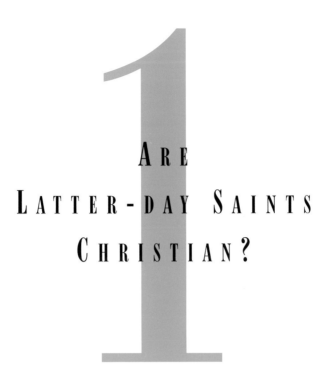

A R E
L A T T E R - D A Y   S A I N T S
C H R I S T I A N ?

THE CHURCH OF JESUS CHRIST OF LATTER-DAY SAINTS HAS ALWAYS ACCEPTED Jesus of Nazareth as testified of in the Bible: the divine Redeemer and Son of God who atoned for the sins of all mankind and ensured our universal resurrection. The church has never ceased to affirm that there is no other name given whereby man can be saved (see Acts 4:12). Another book that the church reveres as scripture, the Book of Mormon, declares on its title page that it was written "to the convincing of the Jew and Gentile that Jesus is the Christ, the Eternal God, manifesting himself unto all nations."

In LDS belief, Joseph Smith is the prophet through whom God restored the Church of Christ and named it the Church of Jesus Christ of Latter-day Saints. He stated that "the fundamental principles of our religion are the testimony of the Apostles and Prophets, concerning Jesus Christ, that He died, was buried, and rose again the third day, and ascended into heaven; and all other things which pertain to our religion are only appendages to it."[1] Members of the restored Church of Jesus Christ gratefully rejoice in Christ's atonement, confidently anticipate his glorious return, expect to be brought before him when he judges the entire human race, and hope to dwell with

Detail from Suffer the Little
Children to Come unto Me,
by Carl Heinrich Bloch.

1

him for all eternity. Surely all who profess such beliefs can lay claim to being called Christians.

Obviously there are doctrinal differences between Mormons and people of a variety of other Christian denominations. But Latter-day Saints believe that it must be possible for people to have different points of view and still be Christians. Given the large number of Christian denominations, all of whom disagree on points large and small, this conclusion is inescapable. Latter-day Saints embrace as fellow Christians those who profess faith in Jesus Christ. In the same vein, they believe that no doctrinal difference or variation in practice can loom so large as to cancel out their own sincere belief in and commitment to Jesus Christ as Lord and Redeemer.

DEFINITIONS

Latter-day Saint beliefs are in harmony with what the Bible calls Christian. The terms *Christian* or *Christians* occur only three times in the New Testament (at Acts 11:26; 26:28; and 1 Peter 4:16). In each case these terms simply refer to those who follow Christ, which applies fully to Latter-day Saints.

Members of the restored Church of Jesus Christ of Latter-day Saints fail to find other definitions of Christianity persuasive—definitions based on interpretations of the Bible by particular denominations or on the interpretations of the classical creeds from the early Christian centuries. Latter-day Saints doubt that anyone has the authority to exclude others from Christianity based on these definitions. As C. S. Lewis observed:

> It is not for us to say who, in the deepest sense, is or is not close to the spirit of Christ. We do not see into men's hearts. We cannot judge, and are indeed forbidden to judge. It would be wicked arrogance for us to say that any man is, or is not, a Christian in this refined sense. . . .
>
> . . . When a man who accepts the Christian doctrine lives unworthily of it, it is much clearer to say he is a bad Christian than to say he is not a Christian.[2]

*Members of the restored Church of
Jesus Christ rejoice in Christ's atone-
ment and await his glorious return.
[Painting by Harry Anderson,
The Second Coming]*

Furthermore, any such definitions that would exclude Mormons would expel other groups too—groups that most people would find it very odd to classify as non-Christians. For example, demanding that believers in Christ accept the trinitarian teaching of the Nicene Creed in order to be considered Christians implies that the bishops who voted against that creed at the Council of Nicea were not really Christians. It also questions the Christianity of the many followers of Christ who lived before Nicea, and thus before the full development of classical trinitarian doctrine.

Likewise, Latter-day Saints are puzzled by the declaration that only those people who base their faith and practice exclusively on the sixty-six books of the traditional Protestant biblical canon are Christian—that canonical list was clearly not settled, according to the records of Christian history, until several centuries after the death of Christ, and still is not universally accepted. This definition would banish not only the Latter-day Saints, but also many of the followers of Jesus from the first centuries, about two hundred million Eastern Orthodox Christians, as well as the Roman Catholics who anchor their belief in the authority of apostolic tradition.

A Christian is a person who accepts
Jesus Christ as Lord and Redeemer.
[Painting by Gary L. Kapp, And He
Healed Them Every One]

Consider further the claim that, because Mormons believe salvation to be connected with the authority of a church, they cannot be considered Christians. This claim also defines out of Christendom many of the greatest of the early Christian fathers, to say nothing of the Church of Rome and virtually all of Eastern Christianity.

In other words, definitions of Christianity based on the specific beliefs of one denomination or group of denominations are not very helpful. They often don't take into full account Christian history, and they don't help determine who is or isn't Christian.

HISTORICAL USAGE

The historical fact is that the word *Christian* has been used over the centuries to describe a wide range of practices and theological positions, including some that Latter-day Saints find just as seriously mistaken as do their Protestant critics. For instance, the Marcionites rejected the gospels of Matthew, Mark, and John. The Docetists denied that Christ possessed a real physical body. Yet these groups and many others are routinely referred to as Christians by the scholars who have studied them most.

Christian teachings and practices can be more or less inadequate, even seriously mistaken, while remaining Christian, just as competing theories of the solar system can vary and still lay claim to being scientific theories. The only definition of the word *Christian* that accounts for its use through the centuries and that includes all the individuals and groups who are universally regarded as falling under its description seems to be roughly this: A Christian is a person who accepts Jesus Christ as, uniquely, his or her Lord and Redeemer. By this definition, faithful Latter-day Saints, along with hundreds of millions of other believers in Jesus of Nazareth distributed across many denominations over thousands of years and on every continent, abundantly qualify as Christians.

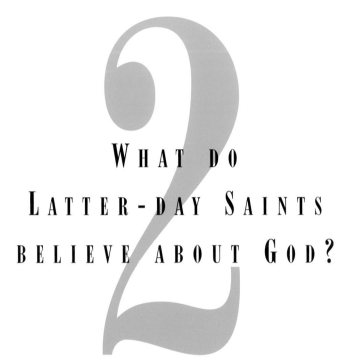

WHAT DO LATTER-DAY SAINTS BELIEVE ABOUT GOD?

THE LATTER-DAY SAINT CONCEPT OF GOD, LIKE THAT OF OTHER CHRISTIANS, is rooted in what the Father has revealed about himself to his prophets and apostles, as well as in what can be learned about him from the earthly life and ministry of Jesus Christ.

With the vast majority of their fellow Christians, members of the Church of Jesus Christ of Latter-day Saints believe in a God of love, who has all knowledge and all power (see 1 Nephi 11:22; 2 Nephi 1:15; 2 Nephi 9:20; D&C 38:1–3; Moses 1:6; 1 Nephi 7:12; Alma 26:35). His continued dealings with the world and with his children in it are chronicled in all four of the canonized "standard works" of the restored Church of Jesus Christ (i.e., the Bible, the Book of Mormon, the Doctrine and Covenants, and the Pearl of Great Price).

Latter-day Saints believe, with other Christians, in three divine persons—the Father, the Son, and the Holy Ghost—and they believe that they are three separate persons (see Matthew 28:19; 2 Nephi 31:21; Alma 11:44; Articles of Faith 1:1). The accounts of Jesus' baptism at the hand of John the Baptist, for example, report that when Jesus emerged from the

The First Vision, by Ted Henninger.

7

John the Baptist Baptizing Jesus,
by Greg K. Olsen.

Jordan River, the Spirit of God descended like a dove from the sky, while the Father's "voice from heaven" testified to the divine sonship of Jesus (see Matthew 3:13–17; Mark 1:9–11; Luke 3:21–22). The New Testament Gospels record several statements from Jesus indicating that he saw himself as separate from God the Father and subordinate to him (see, for example, John 14:28; Matthew 20:23; 26:39; John 5:19; 8:17–18; 17:1–5). In its opening verses in the original Greek, John's Gospel appears to distinguish between the Father, who is "*the* God" *(ho theós)* and the Son, who is "God" *(theós)*. The apostle Paul occasionally reserved the term *God* uniquely for the Father (as in 1 Corinthians 8:6).

> **L**atter-day Saints see the unity of the Godhead in the absolute oneness of purpose and will that characterizes Father, Son, and Holy Ghost.

Latter-day Saints believe that Jesus, too, is divine (see John 1:1; 20:28). Paul wrote of Christ that "in him dwelleth all the fulness of the Godhead bodily" (Colossians 2:9). The scriptures also teach, and Latter-day Saints therefore believe, that the Father, Son, and Holy Ghost are one (see 2 Nephi 31:21; Mosiah 15:4; Alma 11:44; 3 Nephi 11:36; Mormon 7:7; D&C 20:28). "I and my Father are one," said the Savior, declaring further that "the Father is in me" (John 10:30, 38).

ONE OR THREE?

How can this be? How can there be one God, yet three divine persons? Christian thinkers have wrestled with this issue for many centuries. The solution accepted by most Christians was reached through negotiations and debates in the great councils that were held over several centuries following the death of the apostles and their disciples. Borrowing concepts from the era's most advanced thought, Greek philosophy, these Christian theologians attempted to describe the unity-in-multiplicity of the Godhead in philosophical terms.

Latter-day Saints, by contrast, guided not by philosophers but by modern prophets and apostles, see the unity of the Godhead in the absolute oneness of purpose and will that characterizes Father, Son, and Holy Ghost. Jesus sought to establish this same oneness among his disciples. In his famous prayer, the Savior implored "that they all may be one; as thou, Father, art in me, and I in thee, that they also may be one in us . . . that they may be one, even as we are one: I in them, and thou in me, that they may be made perfect in one" (John 17:21–23).

Latter-day Saints understand that God is literally the Father of the spirits of every human being (see Numbers 16:22; 27:16; Matthew 6:9; Ephesians 4:6; Hebrews 12:9). "For," as the apostle Paul told the Athenians, "we are . . . his offspring" (Acts 17:28; compare 17:29). Because we are the children of such a Father, the Savior admonishes us to live up to our heritage, to "be . . . perfect, even as [our] Father which is in heaven is perfect" (Matthew 5:48; compare 3 Nephi 12:48; 27:27; 28:10).

Because God is our Father, Latter-day Saints believe, he is not merely some distant judge who holds us to an abstract standard of justice. Far more perfectly than even the best mortal parents, he loves us and is concerned with our happiness and welfare (see Matthew 7:7–11). "For behold," he told Moses, "this is my work and my glory—to bring to pass the immortality and eternal life of man" (Moses 1:39).

Moreover, because he took upon himself mortal flesh and dwelt among us, our Redeemer, Jesus Christ, the Son of the Father, understands us in all our human weaknesses, trials, and sorrows. The ancient Book of Mormon prophet Alma taught that Jesus would come to earth and submit himself to death and suffering, "that his bowels may be filled with mercy, according to the flesh, that he may know according to the flesh how to succor his people according to their infirmities" (Alma 7:12). Both the New Testament and modern revelation received through the Prophet Joseph Smith testify that Christ's earthly mission was a triumphant success: "For we have not an high priest which cannot be touched with the feeling of our infirmities; but was in all points tempted like as we are, yet without sin" (Hebrews 4:15). "He descended below all things, in that he comprehended all things, that he might be in all and through all things, the light of truth; which truth shineth" (D&C 88:6–7).

GOD'S PHYSICAL FORM

Latter-day Saints take literally the many passages in the Bible that describe God as having a physical form. God created Adam "in his own image" and "after [his] likeness" (Genesis 1:26–27), and Paul taught that ordinary mortal men were in the "image" of God (1 Corinthians 11:7). During his earthly life, Jesus Christ was said to be "the express image" of God the Father (Hebrews 1:3). When the Father and the Son appeared to Joseph Smith in the grove in 1820, the young boy "saw two glorious personages, who exactly resembled each other in features and likeness."[3]

> Latter-day Saints take literally the many passages in the Bible that describe God as having a physical form.

OUR RELATIONSHIP WITH GOD

Thus, for Latter-day Saints God is both near and distant. He is perfect. We are not. He is infinitely loving, just, merciful, and wise. We are not. He has all power and glory. We certainly do not. But he is our Father, we are akin to him, and he wants to share with us all that he has and is. "To him that overcometh," said the Savior, "will I grant to sit with me in my throne, even as I also overcame, and am set down with my Father in his throne" (Revelation 3:21). Accordingly, believers in the restored gospel are filled with love for God their Father, with deep gratitude and divinely inspired hope. "Beloved," wrote the apostle John, "now are we the sons of God, and it doth not yet appear what we shall be: but we know that, when he shall appear, we shall be like him; for we shall see him as he is" (1 John 3:2).

DO LATTER-DAY SAINTS BELIEVE IN THE BIBLE AND BIBLICAL CHRISTIANITY?

THE CHURCH OF JESUS CHRIST OF LATTER-DAY SAINTS ACCEPTS AND HONORS the Bible as the word of God. Latter-day Saints treasure its inspired accounts of the Savior's life and earthly ministry. They read the Bible regularly and accept both the Old and New Testaments among the standard works of the restored Church of Jesus Christ.

Latter-day Saints believe in and strive to live according to the same religion that existed in the church established two thousand years ago by Jesus Christ. They believe that the LDS Church is the restoration of that Church of Christ, restored by the Savior himself. They believe that it teaches all of the doctrines, promotes the virtues, participates in the essential ordinances (sacraments), and is organized according to the principles taught by Jesus and his apostles in the New Testament.

Why do Latter-day Saints believe the Bible? There are many answers to this question. They love the Bible for its own sake. It is a divine witness of Jesus Christ, the Son of God. It contains the words of prophets who spoke of the Savior's coming and his atoning sacrifice. It records the teachings, doctrines, laws, ordinances, and covenants given by God to people over many centuries. Mormons also believe the Bible because the Book of Mormon and other modern revelations affirm that it is true (see Mormon 7:9; D&C 20:11).

INTERPRETATION

Latter-day Saints believe that the guidance of the Holy Ghost is necessary in order to correctly understand the scriptures. This requirement applies equally to the Bible, the Book of Mormon, and modern revelations.

Every Bible-believing Christian church, whether Catholic, Orthodox, Protestant, Evangelical, or Latter-day Saint, interprets the biblical text differently. In interpreting the Bible, some churches rely heavily on tradition; others draw on logic, semantics, philosophy, theory, or history. Members of the restored church believe truth can be found in all of the world's religions but that God has called modern prophets beginning with Joseph Smith and given them revelations to help people understand his word found in the Bible and other sacred writings. In interpreting the Bible, Latter-day Saints strive to rely primarily on the Holy Ghost and the spirit of prophecy and revelation.

Latter-day Saints recognize that the Bible must be translated correctly in order for it to be understood properly in our day, for Jesus did not speak English, either modern or Elizabethan, or any of the other languages found in today's popular Bible translations. This recognition, however, does not hinder Latter-day Saint belief in the Bible, for divine guidance again provides answers in important situations. While the Joseph Smith Translation of the Bible affirms and adopts most of the traditional readings of the King James translation, it also restores explanations and nuances of meaning.

USE OF THE BIBLE

Some people do not know how pervasive the Bible is in the LDS faith and way of life. For example, Latter-day Saints believe in the divinity of Christ, the miracle of grace as taught by Paul (see Ephesians 2:8–10; 2 Nephi 25:23), the necessity of works as taught by James (see James 2:19–20; Alma 9:28), the majesty of love as witnessed by John (see 1 John 3:1–2; Moroni 7:45–48), the resurrection of the dead through the Lord Jesus Christ (see 1 Corinthians 15; Helaman 14:15–18), and many other doctrines that are taught in the Bible. Much of the language in the LDS Articles of Faith is drawn from the words of the apostle Paul and other New Testament texts. Several revelations received by Joseph Smith were stimulated by his desire to understand the meaning of passages in the Bible. For example, after reading John 5:29, Joseph Smith asked the Lord concerning the meaning of Jesus' reference to "the resurrection of damnation," and in response Joseph received a resplendent revelation of the three degrees of glory in the world to come (see D&C 76).

The organization of the Church of Jesus Christ of Latter-day Saints follows the model found in the New Testament. The church is led by "apostles and prophets, Jesus Christ himself being the chief corner stone" (Ephesians 2:20), a presidency of three (compare Peter, James, and John), and quorums of seventy to take the gospel to the world (see Luke 10:1). It also contains other offices such as elders, bishops, teachers, deacons, evangelists, and so forth (see Ephesians 4:11; Philippians 1:1; 1 Timothy 5:17; Titus 1:7).

Many LDS practices are also found in the Bible. Latter-day Saints perform the ordinances of the New Testament—the baptism of believers by full immersion in water (see John 3:23; D&C 20:73–74), the laying on of hands to confer the gift of the Holy Ghost (see Acts 8:14–17; Moroni 2), the sacrament of the Lord's Supper (see 1 Corinthians 11:23–25; D&C 20:75–79), and the laying on of hands to confer the priesthood (see 1 Timothy 4:14; Moroni 3), as well as the clearly mentioned but widely misunderstood ordinance of baptism on behalf of people who have died (see 1 Corinthians 15:29; D&C 127–28).

Moreover, Latter-day Saints pay tithing (see Malachi 3:8; Matthew 23:23; D&C 119), call the elders to anoint the sick with oil in the name of the Lord (see James 5:14; D&C 42:43–51), and fast and pray often (see Matthew 6:17–18; Alma 6:6). Even plural marriage (see D&C 132) and the sharing of property in a united order, which were practiced at one time in Mormon history as instructed by God (see D&C 42; 51; 83; 104), find obvious parallels in the Bible (see Genesis 16:1–3; Deuteronomy 21:15; Acts 2:44). In many ways such as these, Latter-day Saints show their belief in the Bible, not only in word or thought but also in deed and action.

Latter-day Saints believe in God the Eternal Father, and in his Son Jesus Christ, and in the Holy Ghost (see Articles of Faith 1:1). They join the apostle Paul in confessing God: "Giving thanks unto the Father, which hath made us meet to be partakers of the inheritance of the saints in light: who hath delivered us from the power of darkness, and hath translated us into the kingdom of his dear Son: in whom we have redemption through his blood, even the forgiveness of sins" (Colossians 1:12–14). Latter-day Saints praise "God our Saviour; who will have all men to be saved, and to come unto the knowledge of the truth. For there is one God, and one mediator between God and men, the man Christ Jesus; who gave himself a ransom for all" (1 Timothy 2:3–6). They salute all the world, hoping that "the grace of the Lord Jesus Christ, and the love of God, and the communion

In Remembrance of Me, by Walter Rane.

of the Holy Ghost" will be with everyone (2 Corinthians 13:14). Such confessions from the Bible are fully embraced by Latter-day Saints.

THE CREEDS

Latter-day Saints believe, however, that the creeds of the later Christian councils did not accurately preserve the biblical doctrine of God. Members of the restored Church of Christ do not recognize the authority of these councils to issue binding formulations of doctrine. Moreover, Latter-day Saints believe that the creeds are not consistent with each other, each becoming more removed from biblical teachings and doctrine as time went by. The earliest form of the Old Roman Creed (from the second century) is fairly simple and close to the Bible. Later forms, however, move step by step away from the Bible. The Caesarean Creed (late third

century) and the received form of the Apostles' Creed confess God the Father—instead of Jesus Christ, as taught in the Bible (see John 1:3; Ephesians 3:9; Hebrews 1:2)—as the "Creator of all things" or "Maker of heaven and earth." The Nicene Creed (fourth century) began to speak of Jesus as being "from the substance of the Father" and "of one substance with the Father," introducing these nonbiblical expressions into the creedal formulas. Eventually, the so-called Athanasian Creed (about the seventh century) added notions such as "one God in Trinity, and Trinity in Unity" and dictated that to be saved a person "must think in this way of the Trinity."[4] Latter-day Saints find certain aspects of these formal creeds to be unbiblical and spiritually limiting. They prefer the testimonies given in the Bible and in modern revelation to the formulations fashioned by councils or synods, however astute they may have been.

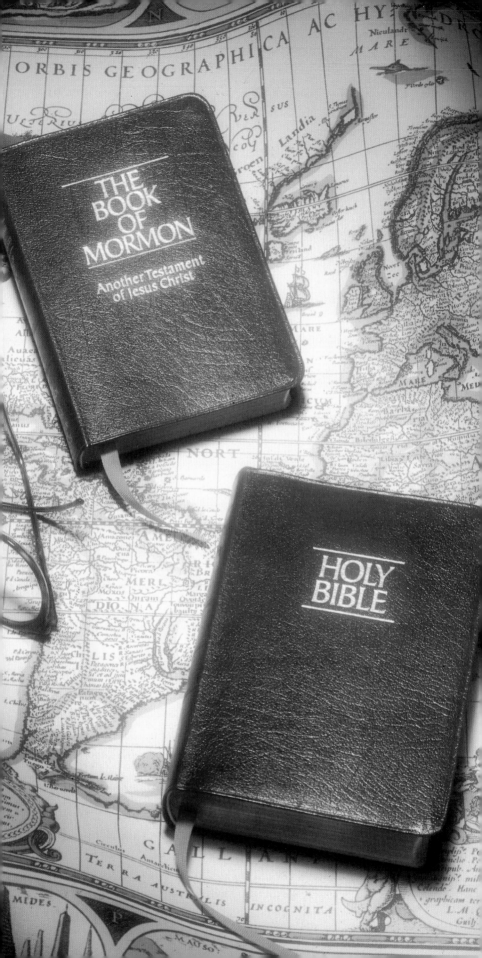

DOES GOD SPEAK TO HIS CHILDREN IN WAYS OTHER THAN THROUGH THE BIBLE?

AS STATED PREVIOUSLY, THE CHURCH OF JESUS CHRIST OF LATTER-DAY SAINTS believes the Bible to be the word of God. Latter-day Saints love and study the Bible and attempt to live according to its teachings. They do not, however, believe that the Bible contains all of God's word to all people of all time.

Joseph Smith loved the Bible. It was through pondering certain verses in the Epistle of James that he felt directed to call upon God in prayer. Most of his sermons, writings, and letters are laced with quotations or summaries of biblical passages and precepts. He once remarked that one can "see God's own handwriting in the sacred volume: and he who reads it oftenest will like it best."[5]

IS IT COMPLETE?

Joseph Smith did not believe, however, that the Bible was complete or that all religious difficulties could necessarily be handled by turning to the Old or New Testaments for help (see Joseph Smith—History 1:12). Nor did he believe in either the inerrancy or the infallibility of the Bible. "From sundry revelations which had been received," he explained, "it was apparent that many important points touching the salvation of men had been taken

Belief that the Book of Mormon also contains the word of God does not diminish Latter-day Saint belief in doctrines found in the Bible.

That Ye May Know, by Gary L. Kapp.

from the Bible, or lost before it was compiled."[6] In like manner, members of the church restored through Joseph Smith today revere the Bible but do not believe that it is without fault or that it contains all of what God has to say to his children.

The ninth article of faith of the Church of Jesus Christ of Latter-day Saints states: "We believe all that God has revealed, all that He does now reveal, and we believe that He will yet reveal many great and important things pertaining to the Kingdom of God." For Latter-day Saints, what God *has* revealed includes the Bible, the Book of Mormon, the Doctrine and Covenants, and the Pearl of Great Price. What he *does now* reveal is the current and ongoing inspired instruction given through those called to lead his church and kingdom on the earth—modern-day apostles and prophets (see D&C 68:1–4). And what he *will yet reveal* includes what he will in the future make known through his chosen leaders.

OTHER SCRIPTURE

The Bible is one of the books within the LDS standard works, and thus doctrines and practices of the Latter-day Saints are in harmony with the Bible. There are times, of course, when latter-day revelation provides clarification or enhancement of the intended meaning in the Bible. But adding to the canon is not the same as rejecting the canon. Supplementation is not the same as contradiction. All the prophets, and the Savior himself, brought new light and knowledge to the world; in many cases, new scripture came as a result of their ministries. That new scripture did not invalidate what went before, nor did it close the door to subsequent revelation.

Belief in other scriptures, including modern-day revelations, does not undermine Latter-day Saint belief in the Bible. Just as Isaiah could add his prophecies to join the books of Moses, and just as Peter's letters complement the writings of Paul, Joseph Smith could add his scriptural voice to that of Elijah, Jeremiah, and John—in each case without undermining faith in the previous scripture.

Likewise, belief that the Book of Mormon also contains the word of God does not diminish Latter-day Saint belief in doctrines found in the Bible. Latter-day Saints believe that both books of scripture go hand in hand, in every way possible. They read Ezekiel 37:15–17 as a biblical prophecy declaring that two holy books would become one in the hands of the righteous in the latter days. The words of LDS Church president Heber J. Grant illustrate the LDS perspective on the Bible: "All my life I have been finding additional evidences that the Bible is the Book of books, and that the Book of Mormon is the greatest witness for the truth of the Bible that has ever been published."[7]

Latter-day Saints agree that the biblical canon is closed—that no new books should become part of the Bible. This does not mean, however, that all scripture is closed or that God, who opens and closes the heavens, cannot and will not continue to reveal his will.

WHY MORE SCRIPTURE?

There are many needs for revelation beyond the Bible. For one thing, many facts remain unreported in the New Testament. For example, on the Mount of Transfiguration and for forty days after his resurrection, Jesus instructed his apostles (see Matthew 17:1–13; Acts 1:1–3). Although the Bible is silent on what happened during these events, Latter-day Saint revelations disclose that Jesus taught his apostles important principles, gave them priesthood authority, and endowed them with spiritual gifts on these occasions. Likewise, the Gospel of John reports that Jesus told the Jews that he had "other sheep" besides them and that these others would also "hear" his voice (see John 10:16). The Book of Mormon reveals how these words of Jesus were literally fulfilled (see 3 Nephi 15:11–24; 16:1–3).

Furthermore, Latter-day revelation provides answers to many practical and doctrinal questions that arise out of the biblical text. From the Bible, many views can be entertained concerning such matters as the nature of God, the purposes of life, the rules of marriage and divorce, and the possibilities for repentance and salvation after death. Complete answers to questions like these are not always found in the Bible alone. Without further revelation, answers to these and similar questions that have been asked over the years remain unsatisfactory.

In addition, Latter-day Saints can see that history has not always been kind to the records of Christianity. Certain plain and precious things have been lost. For example, the apostle Paul wrote other letters that no longer exist (see 1 Corinthians 5:9; Ephesians 3:3), and it is widely believed that Matthew, Mark, and Luke may have relied on an earlier, now missing documentary source as they wrote their Gospels. Latter-day Saints assume that these lost records would be of great value to all Christians. These losses can be attributed, at least in part, to the problems of apostasy and division described in the New Testament itself (see Acts 20:29; 1 Corinthians 11:18; 2 Thessalonians 2:3). Latter-day Saints believe that at least some of these losses have been compensated for by the word of God contained in scriptures brought forth in these latter days.

In the Book of Mormon, to the people known as the Nephites, the Lord said:

> And because my words shall hiss forth—many of the Gentiles shall say: A Bible! A Bible! We have got a Bible, and there cannot be any more Bible. . . .
>
> Thou fool, that shall say: A Bible, we have got a Bible, and we need no more Bible. . . .
>
> Know ye not that there are more nations than one? Know ye not that I, the Lord your God, have created all men, and that I remember those who are upon the isles of the sea; and that I rule in the heavens above and in the earth beneath; and I bring forth my word unto the children of men, yea, even upon all the nations of the earth?
>
> Wherefore murmur ye, because that ye shall receive more of my word? Know ye not that the testimony of two nations is a witness unto you that I am God, that I remember one nation like unto another? . . . And when the two nations shall run together the testimony of the two nations shall run together also.
>
> And I do this that I may prove unto many that I am the same yesterday, today, and forever; and that I speak forth my words according to mine own pleasure. And because that I have spoken one word ye need not suppose that I cannot speak another; for my work is not yet finished; neither shall it be until the end of man, neither from that time henceforth and forever. (2 Nephi 29:3, 6, 7–9)

The need for continual revelation in our day was taught by a former president of the LDS Church, John Taylor:

> We require a living tree—a living fountain—living intelligence, proceeding from the living priesthood in heaven, through the living priesthood on earth. . . . And from the time that Adam first received a communication from God, to the time that John, on the Isle of Patmos, received his communication, or Joseph Smith had the heavens opened to him, it always required new revelations, adapted to the peculiar circumstances in which the churches or individuals were placed. Adam's revelation did not instruct Noah to build his ark; nor did Noah's revelation tell Lot to forsake Sodom; nor did either of these speak of the departure of the children of Israel from Egypt. These all had revelations for themselves, and so had Isaiah, Jeremiah, Ezekiel, Jesus, Peter, Paul, John, and Joseph. And so must we, or we shall make a shipwreck.[8]

Those who appeal to Revelation 22:18–19 as evidence that there is to be no revelation beyond the Bible should keep in mind that those verses could not have been meant to refer to the Bible itself, because the Bible as we have it today was not yet compiled when John the Revelator wrote those words. Instead, John was proclaiming the eternal principle that no uninspired mortal is to "add unto" or "take away from" revelations from God; such revelations are to be accepted and obeyed as given. This same principle is taught in Deuteronomy 4:2, 3 Nephi 11:40, and Doctrine and Covenants 20:35.

God loves all his children and does not leave them without guidance. In addition to the official, canonized revelations we know as scripture, Latter-day Saints believe that God has made available to every individual a means by which his will can be known. There is a "power of God" called the "light of Christ" that "proceedeth forth from the presence of God to fill the immensity of space" (D&C 88:7, 12, 13). This power "giveth light to every man that cometh into the world" and "enlighteneth every man . . . that hearkeneth" to it (D&C 84:46). The promise is that anyone who will listen to and obey the promptings of this power will be brought unto God and eventually led to the fulness of the gospel of Jesus Christ (see D&C 84:47–48; Moroni 7:16–20). In addition, those who repent and are baptized are given an additional gift— the gift of the Holy Ghost. This gift can bring personal revelation as well as all the other wonderful gifts of the Spirit spoken of in the scriptures.

Do Latter-day Saints Believe That Men and Women Can Become Gods?

MEMBERS OF THE CHURCH OF JESUS CHRIST OF LATTER-DAY SAINTS BELIEVE that human beings can grow and progress spiritually until, through the mercy and grace of Christ, they can inherit and possess all that the Father has—they can become gods. This is taught in revelations given to modern prophets (see D&C 76:58; 132:19–20), as well as in sermons delivered by Joseph Smith.[9] A couplet written by Lorenzo Snow, fifth president of the LDS Church, states:

As man now is, God once was;
As God now is, man may be.[10]

This doctrine is generally referred to as deification, and the LDS expression of this doctrine is often misrepresented and misunderstood. Latter-day Saints do not believe that human beings will ever be independent of God, or that they will ever cease to be subordinate to God. They believe that to become as God means to overcome the world through the atonement of Jesus Christ (see 1 John 5:4–5; Revelation 2:7, 11). Thus the faithful become heirs of God and joint heirs with Christ and will inherit *all*

The Grand Council, by Robert T. Barrett.

things just as Christ inherits all things (see Romans 8:17; Galatians 4:7; 1 Corinthians 3:21–23; Revelation 21:7). They are received into the "church of the firstborn," meaning they inherit as though they were the firstborn (see Hebrews 12:23). There are no limitations on these scriptural declarations; those who become as God shall inherit *all* things. In that glorified state they will resemble our Savior; they will receive his glory and be one with him and with the Father (see 1 John 3:2; 1 Corinthians 15:49; 2 Corinthians 3:18; John 17:21–23; Philippians 3:21).

ANCIENT DOCTRINE

The doctrine of the deification of man is not an exclusive teaching of the restored Church of Jesus Christ. Rather, it can be found in early Christian history. In the second century, Irenaeus, bishop of Lyons (about A.D. 130–200), the most important Christian theologian of his time, said much the same thing as Lorenzo Snow:

> If the Word became a man,
> It was so men may become gods.[11]

Further, Irenaeus asked:

> Do we cast blame on him [God] because we were not made gods from the beginning, but were at first created merely as men, and then later as gods? Although God has adopted this course out of his pure benevolence, that no one may charge him with discrimination or stinginess, he declares, "I have said, Ye are gods; and all of you are sons of the Most High." . . . For it was necessary at first that nature be exhibited, then after that what was mortal would be conquered and swallowed up in immortality.[12]

At about the same time, Clement of Alexandria (about A.D. 150–215) wrote: "Yea, I say, the Word of God became a man so that you might learn from a man how to become a god."[13] Clement also said that "if one knows himself, he will know God, and knowing God will become like God. . . . His is beauty, true beauty, for it is God, and that man becomes a god, since God wills it. So Heraclitus was right when he said, 'Men are gods, and gods are men.'"[14]

Still in the second century, Justin Martyr (about A.D. 100–165) insisted that in the beginning men "were made like God, free from suffering and death," and that they are thus "deemed worthy of becoming gods and of having power to become sons of the highest."[15] Athanasius, bishop of

Latter-day Saints do not believe that human beings will ever be independent of God, or that they will ever cease to be subordinate to God. They believe that to become as God means to overcome the world through the atonement of Jesus Christ. [Painting by Del Parson, He Is Risen]

Alexandria (about A.D. 296–373), also stated his belief in deification in terms very similar to those of Lorenzo Snow: "The Word was made flesh in order that we might be enabled to be made gods. . . . Just as the Lord, putting on the body, became a man, so also we men are both deified through his flesh, and henceforth inherit everlasting life."[16] On another occasion Athanasius observed: "He became man that we might be made divine."[17] Finally, Augustine of Hippo (A.D. 354–430), the greatest of the early Christian Fathers, said: "But he himself that justifies also deifies, for by justifying he makes sons of God. 'For he has given them power to become the sons of God' [John 1:12]. If then we have been made sons of god, we have also been made gods."[18]

All five of the above writers were not just orthodox Christians, but also in time became revered as saints. Three of the five wrote within a hundred years of the period of the apostles, and all five believed in the doctrine of deification. This doctrine was a part of historical Christianity until relatively recent times, and it is still an important doctrine in some

Eastern Orthodox churches. One writer states that a fundamental principle of orthodoxy in the patristic period was recognizing "the history of the universe as the history of divinization and salvation." As a result the early Christian Fathers concluded that "because the Spirit is truly God, we are truly divinized by the presence of the Spirit."[19]

The Westminster Dictionary of Christian Theology contains the following in an article titled "Deification":

> Deification (Greek *theosis*) is for Orthodoxy the goal of every Christian. Man, according to the Bible, is 'made in the image and likeness of God.'. . . It is possible for man to become like God, to become deified, to become god by grace. This doctrine is based on many passages of both OT and NT (e.g. Ps. 82 (81).6; II Peter 1.4), and it is essentially the teaching both of St Paul, though he tends to use the language of filial adoption (cf. Rom. 8.9–17; Gal. 4.5–7), and the Fourth Gospel (cf. 17.21–23).
>
> The language of II Peter is taken up by St Irenaeus, in his famous phrase, 'if the Word has been made man, it is so that men may be made gods' (*Adv. Haer* V, Pref.), and becomes the standard in Greek theology. In the fourth century St Athanasius repeats Irenaeus almost word for word, and in the fifth century St Cyril of Alexandria says that we shall become sons 'by participation' (Greek *methexis*). Deification is the central idea in the spirituality of St Maximus the Confessor, for whom the doctrine is the corollary of the Incarnation: 'Deification, briefly, is the encompassing and fulfillment of all times and ages,' . . . and St Symeon the New Theologian at the end of the tenth century writes, 'He who is God by nature converses with those whom he has made gods by grace, as a friend converses with his friends, face to face.' . . .
>
> Finally, it should be noted that deification does not mean absorption into God, since the deified creature remains itself and distinct. It is the whole human being, body and soul, who is transfigured in the Spirit into the likeness of the divine nature, and deification is the goal of every Christian.[20]

In short, whether one accepts or rejects the doctrine of the deification of man, it was clearly a part of mainstream Christian orthodoxy for centuries. Joseph Smith obviously did not make it up. Instead, Latter-day Saints believe, it is an eternal truth restored through modern prophets.

In the LDS view, those who are worthy will receive the full divine inheritance only through the atonement of Christ and only after having received a glorious resurrection. Closer to the Latter-day Saint understanding of the doctrine are the views expressed by C. S. Lewis, whose genuine Christianity is virtually undisputed: "It is a serious thing to live in a society of possible gods and goddesses, to remember that the dullest and most uninteresting person you talk to may one day be a creature which, if you saw it now, you would be strongly tempted to worship."[21]

In a fuller statement of this doctrine of deification, Lewis explained:

> The command *Be ye perfect* is not idealistic gas. Nor is it a command to do the impossible. He is going to make us into creatures that can obey that command. He said (in the Bible) that we were "gods" and He is going to make good His words. If we let Him—for we can prevent Him, if we choose—He will make the feeblest and filthiest of us into a god or goddess, dazzling, radiant, immortal creature, pulsating all through with such energy and joy and wisdom and love as we cannot now imagine, a bright stainless mirror which reflects back to God perfectly (though, of course, on a smaller scale) His own boundless power and delight and goodness. The process will be long and in parts very painful; but that is what we are in for. Nothing less. He meant what He said.[22]

God and Christ are the objects of LDS worship. Even though Mormons believe in the ultimate deification of man, nothing in LDS literature speaks of worshipping any being other than the Father and the Son. Latter-day Saints believe in "one God" in the sense that they love and serve one Godhead, each member of which possesses all of the attributes of godhood.

Since the scriptures teach that those who gain eternal life will look like God, receive the inheritance of God, receive the glory of God, be one with God, sit upon the throne of God, and exercise the power and rule of God, then surely it cannot be un-Christian to conclude with C. S. Lewis and others that such beings as these can be *called* gods, as long as we remember that this use of the term *gods* does not in any way reduce or limit the sovereignty of God our Father. That is how the early Christians used the term; it is how C. S. Lewis used the term; and it is how Latter-day Saints use the term and understand the doctrine.

WHAT DO LATTER-DAY SAINTS MEAN WHEN THEY SAY THAT GOD WAS ONCE A MAN?

JOSEPH SMITH TAUGHT IN APRIL 1844:

> God himself was once as we are now, and is an exalted man, and sits enthroned in yonder heavens! That is the great secret. If the veil were rent today, and the great God who holds this world in its orbit, and who upholds all worlds and all things by His power, was to make himself visible,—I say, if you were to see him today, you would see him like a man in form—like yourselves in all the person, image, and very form as a man. . . .
>
> . . . It is the first principle of the gospel to know for a certainty the character of God, and to know that we may converse with Him as one man converses with another, and that He was once a man like us; yea, that God himself, the Father of us all, dwelt on an earth, the same as Jesus Christ Himself did.[23]

As we have seen, Lorenzo Snow, fifth president of the LDS Church, summarized this doctrine in a couplet: "As man now is, God once was; As God now is, man may be."[24]

Detail from *The First Vision,*
by Gary L. Kapp.

In proclaiming this doctrine, neither Joseph Smith nor his successors have in any way sought to limit or degrade the Almighty. In fact, both the Book of Mormon and the Doctrine and Covenants state emphatically that there is no knowledge or power or divine attribute that God does not possess in perfection. "O how great the holiness of our God! For he knoweth all things, and there is not anything save he knows it" (2 Nephi 9:20; see 2 Nephi 2:24; Moroni 7:22). He truly "has all power, all wisdom, and all understanding" (Alma 26:35). He who is "mightier than all the earth" (1 Nephi 4:1) "comprehendeth all things, and all things are before him" (D&C 88:41). Mormons accept the reality that "there is a God in heaven, who is infinite and eternal, from everlasting to everlasting the same unchangeable God, the framer of heaven and earth, and all things which are in them" (D&C 20:17).

MORTALITY

That God was once a mortal being is in no way inconsistent with the fact that he now has all power and all knowledge and possesses every virtue, grace, and godly attribute. He acquired perfection through long periods of growth, development, and progression, "by going from one small degree to another, and from a small capacity to a great one; from grace to grace, from exaltation to exaltation," as Joseph Smith explained. "When you climb up a ladder, you must begin at the bottom, and ascend step by step, until you arrive at the top; and so it is with the principles of the gospel—you must begin with the first, and go on until you learn all the principles of exaltation. But it will be a great while after you have passed through the veil before you will have learned them. It is not all to be comprehended in this world; it will be a great work to learn our salvation and exaltation even beyond the grave."[25]

FROM EVERLASTING TO EVERLASTING

How, then, do Latter-day Saints reconcile the scriptural description of God as being "from everlasting to everlasting" with the idea that he has not always been God? For one thing, they believe that biblical passages that speak of God's eternality and of his being the same yesterday, today, and forever make reference to his divine attributes—his love, constancy, and willingness to bless his people (see, for example, Psalm 102:27; Hebrews 1:12; 13:8). Such passages are also found in the Book of Mormon and the Doctrine and Covenants and, again, refer to God's divine nature (see 1 Nephi 10:18–19; 2 Nephi 27:23; Alma 7:20; Mormon 9:8–11, 19; Moroni 8:18; 10:7; D&C 3:2; 20:12, 17; 35:1).

Not much has been revealed about this concept beyond the fact that

God was once a man and that over a long period of time he gained the knowledge, power, and divine attributes necessary to know all things and have all power. Because he has held his exalted status for a longer period than any of us can conceive, he is able to speak in terms of eternity and can state that he is from everlasting to everlasting. President Joseph Fielding Smith explained that "from eternity to eternity means from the spirit existence through the probation which we are in, and then back again to the eternal existence which will follow. Surely this is everlasting, for when we receive the resurrection, we will never die. We all existed in the first eternity. I think I can say of myself and others, we are from eternity; and we will be to eternity everlasting, if we receive the exaltation."[26]

EMPATHY

President Brigham Young taught that our Father in Heaven "has passed the ordeals we are now passing through; he has received an experience, has suffered and enjoyed, and knows all that we know regarding the toils, sufferings, life and death of this mortality, for he has passed through the whole of it, and has received his crown and exaltation."[27] Men and women can thus relate to him as a father and pray to him with the perfect assurance that he understands our struggles. His experience contributes to his empathy as well as to his omniscient and all-loving capacity to judge his children. President Young observed that "it must be that God knows something about temporal things, and has had a body and been on an earth, were it not so He would not know how to judge men righteously, according to the temptations and sin they have had to contend with."[28]

For Latter-day Saints, God is far more than the ultimate cosmic force or primal cause; he is a personal being, an exalted Man of Holiness, literally our Father in Heaven (see Moses 6:57). He has a body, parts, and passions. He is approachable, knowable, and, like his Beloved Son, able to be touched with the feeling of our infirmities (see Hebrews 4:15). He has tender regard for his children and desires that we become as he is—not through our personal effort alone, but primarily through the mercy, grace, and transforming and glorifying power that come through the atonement of Jesus Christ.

These doctrines are not clearly stated in the Bible. Mormons believe, however, that this knowledge was once had among the ancients and that it has been restored through modern prophets. To those who sincerely seek an understanding of their true selves and destiny, latter-day prophets have affirmed that through truly coming to know God, men and women may come to understand their own eternal identities and divine possibilities. In the words of Joseph Smith, "If men do not comprehend the character of God, they do not comprehend themselves."[29]

7

WHAT DO LATTER-DAY SAINTS BELIEVE A PERSON MUST DO TO BE SAVED?

JOSEPH SMITH WROTE IN 1842: "WE BELIEVE THAT THROUGH THE Atonement of Christ, all mankind may be saved, by obedience to the laws and ordinances of the Gospel" (Articles of Faith 1:3). From an LDS perspective, no person who comes to earth is outside the reach of Christ's power to save, no soul beyond the pale of mercy and grace. No one came to earth either predestined to be saved or denied the right to the same. God is no respecter of persons, "but in every nation he that feareth him, and worketh righteousness, is accepted with him" (Acts 10:34–35).

IMMORTALITY AND ETERNAL LIFE

In the Pearl of Great Price are recorded the following words of God to Moses: "For behold, this is my work and my glory—to bring to pass the immortality and eternal life of man" (Moses 1:39). This is a capsule statement, a distillation and summary of the work of redemption in Christ. Mormons believe there are two types of salvation made available through the atonement of Jesus Christ—universal and individual. All who receive a physical body—whether they are good or bad, evil or righteous—will be resurrected (see 1 Corinthians 15:22; Alma 11:41). This universal

The Crucifixion, by Carl Heinrich Bloch.

salvation from physical death is the *immortality* spoken of in the book of Moses. It is salvation from the grave, or endless life. It is a universal gift.

Individual salvation is another matter. Though all salvation is made possible through the mercy and love of Christ, Mormons believe there are certain things individuals must do for divine grace to be fully activated in their lives. That is, they must willingly receive the Lord's gift, which is freely given. People must come unto him—accept him as Lord and Savior, have faith on his name, repent of sin, be baptized, receive the gift of the Holy Ghost, and strive to remain faithful to the end of their days. *Eternal life* comes to those who believe, obey, and endure to the end. Christ is "the author of eternal salvation unto all them that obey him" (Hebrews 5:9). Eternal life is endless life, but it is also life with God. It is God's life. It is the highest form of salvation.

GRACE AND WORKS

Coming unto Christ represents a covenant, a two-way promise between God and man. Jesus Christ has done for us what we could never do for ourselves. He suffered and bled and died for us. He redeems us from sin. He offers to change our nature, to make us into new creatures (see 2 Corinthians 5:17; Mosiah 27:24–26). He rose from the dead and thereby opened the door for us to do the same at the appointed time. These things we could not do for ourselves; they are acts of mercy and grace. Our promise is to accept Christ as our Savior, be faithful to our covenants, obey his commandments, and endure to the end.

Etching by Carl Heinrich Bloch.

Latter-day Saints readily acknowledge that though our efforts to be righteous are *necessary*, they will never be *sufficient* to save us. Book of Mormon prophets thus explained that above and beyond all we can do, we are saved by the grace of Christ and that our most significant labor is to trust in and rely upon the merits and mercy and grace of the Holy Messiah (see 2 Nephi 10:24; 25:23; 2 Nephi 2:8; 31:19; Moroni 6:4).

Unfortunately, the theological debate over whether we are saved by grace or by works has continued for centuries. It is, as C. S. Lewis observed, "like asking which blade in a pair of scissors is most necessary."[30] Few things would reveal the shallowness of one's discipleship more than giving lip service to God while avoiding wholehearted obedience. True faith always results in faithfulness, faithful action (see James 2). On the other hand, few things are more offensive to God than trusting solely in one's own works, relying upon one's own strength, and seeking to prosper through one's own genius.

THE ATONEMENT OF CHRIST

Christ is the source of our strength and our salvation. "How else could salvation possibly come?" asked Elder Bruce R. McConkie, a former apostle in the LDS Church. "Can man save himself? Can he resurrect himself? Can he create a celestial kingdom and decree his own admission thereto? Salvation must and does originate with God, and if man is to receive it, God must bestow it upon him, which bestowal is a manifestation of grace. . . . Salvation is in Christ and comes through his atonement."[31] Or as Elder Dallin H. Oaks, another Latter-day Saint apostle, observed: "Man unquestionably has impressive powers and can bring to pass great things by tireless efforts and indomitable will. But after all our obedience and good works, we cannot be saved from the effect of our sins without the grace extended by the atonement of Jesus Christ."[32]

Joseph Smith learned by revelation that the greatest blessings in the world to come are reserved for those who come unto Christ, accept his gospel, receive the necessary sacraments or ordinances, and remain true to their covenants. Those who do these things inherit the fulness of the glory of God (see D&C 76; 132:19). The Prophet Joseph later revealed the importance of temples as sacred places wherein the children of God can

> Salvation must and does originate with God, and if man is to receive it, God must bestow it upon him, which bestowal is a manifestation of grace. . . . Salvation is in Christ and comes through his atonement.
>
> BRUCE R. MCCONKIE

The instruction and ordinances received in Latter-day Saint temples are centered in Christ. [San Diego Temple. Photo by David C. Gaunt]

participate in ordinances that bind and seal families for time and all eternity (see D&C 131–32). The instruction and ordinances of the temple are remarkably Christ-centered and continue to provide the ever-needed reminder that without him we have no hope of peace and happiness here and no claim on eternal glory hereafter.

Words like *salvation, exaltation,* and *eternal life* are often used in LDS religious discourse. In essence, each of these words means the same thing, but each lays stress upon different aspects of the saved condition. The word *salvation* emphasizes one's saved condition, the deliverance from death and sin through the atoning sacrifice of Jesus Christ. *Eternal* is one of the names of God, and thus to possess eternal life is to enjoy God's life. The word *exaltation* lays stress upon the elevated and ennobled status of one who qualifies for the society of the redeemed and glorified in the celestial kingdom.

Modern Revelation

Latter-day Saints rejoice in the knowledge of a plan of salvation that has come to them through modern prophets—vital knowledge of matters that continue to be debated in the Christian world, such as:

- who we are—where we came from, why we are here, and where we are going after death;
- to what degree our faith in Christ must be manifest in our faithfulness to his commandments;
- the status of those who die without a knowledge of Christ and his gospel.

Joseph Smith taught that for a man to be saved is to be "placed beyond the power of all his enemies."[33] Even though the ultimate blessings of salvation do not come until the next life, there is a sense in which people in this life may enjoy the assurance of salvation and the peace that accompanies that knowledge (see D&C 59:23). The Holy Spirit provides the "earnest of our inheritance," the promise or certification that we are on course and thus in line for full salvation in the world to come (see 2 Corinthians 1:21–22; 5:5; Ephesians 1:13–14). If we are doing all we can to cultivate the gifts of the Spirit, we are living in what might be called a saved condition. LDS Church president David O. McKay thus observed that "the gospel of Jesus Christ, as revealed to the Prophet Joseph Smith, is in very deed, in every way, the power of God unto salvation. It is salvation *here*—here and now. It gives to every man the perfect life, here and now, as well as hereafter."[34]

D o   t h e   D o c t r i n e s   a n d   p r a c t i c e s   o f   t h e   L D S   C h u r c h   c h a n g e ?

SOME MAY SEE CHANGE IN TEACHINGS AND PRACTICES AS AN INCONSISTENCY or weakness, but to Latter-day Saints change is a sign of the very foundation of strength upon which the Church of Jesus Christ of Latter-day Saints is built—that God is always (yesterday, today, and forever) willing to reveal his will to his people if they are willing to listen and obey. Although the eternal saving principles of God's plan of salvation for his children do not change, the revelation of those principles and their application—to whom, when, where, how much—varies to meet a myriad of mortal circumstances and God's purposes and timetable.

Members of the restored Church of Jesus Christ believe that there are many great and important things yet to be revealed (see Articles of Faith 1:9); this indicates that our past and current understanding of things is incomplete and may need adjustment.

LINE UPON LINE

But why doesn't God give us everything we will ever need to know and be done with it? Because God honors both agency and circumstance and reveals his will as his children are willing and able to receive it and as it is appropriate to fulfill his own purposes. Isaiah taught this principle:

> Whom shall he teach knowledge? and whom shall he make to understand doctrine? them that are weaned from the milk, and drawn from the breasts.
>
> For precept must be upon precept, precept upon precept; line upon line, line upon line; here a little, and there a little. (Isaiah 28:9–10)

This principle is illustrated clearly in the New Testament in terms of an important change in policy or practice in the early Christian church. When Jesus called and first sent out his twelve apostles, he said: "Go not into the way of the Gentiles, and into any city of the Samarians enter ye not: But go rather to the lost sheep of the house of Israel" (Matthew 10:5–6). Years later Jesus revealed to Peter that it was time for a change. The gospel was now to go to the Gentiles. It took a repeated revelation and a remarkable demonstration of the power of God to convince Peter that this significant change in direction was to be made (see Acts 10).

A LIVING CHURCH

And so it has been in our own day. Latter-day Saints acknowledge change as an integral part of the living church, a vital dimension of what it means to be led by living prophets. The need for revelation to properly apply the truths of heaven was taught by Joseph Smith in these words:

> God said, "Thou shalt not kill;" at another time He said, "Thou shalt utterly destroy." This is the principle on which the government of heaven is conducted—by revelation adapted to the circumstances in which the children of the kingdom are placed. Whatever God commands is right, no matter what it is, although we may not see the reason thereof till long after the events transpire. . . .
>
> . . . As God has designed our happiness—and the happiness of all His creatures, he never has—He never will institute an ordinance or give a commandment to His people that is not calculated in its nature to promote that happiness which He has designed, and which will not end in the greatest amount of good and glory to those who become the recipients of his law and ordinances.[35]

If such changes were to come by the whims of mortals, there would be serious cause for concern. If those changes come, however, by revelation from God to his duly authorized servants, they are right and God's people are duty bound to accept and obey them.

Globally and historically the principle of growing line upon line is illustrated in God's revealing to various peoples the measure of light and truth they would accept and from which they could benefit. Therefore, it is not surprising to find varying amounts of gospel truth among all cultures, philosophical systems, world religions, and the many Christian churches existing in the world. Some, in fact, enjoy much of the gospel of Jesus Christ, and their adherents are wonderful examples of Christian living. However, Latter-day Saints believe that there is something called the "fulness of the gospel" that is available to those who desire it. That fulness was restored to the earth through Joseph Smith and is proclaimed by the Church of Jesus Christ of Latter-day Saints. It includes belief in living prophets who are called by God and to whom he reveals his will. These prophets and others ordained by them have authority to preach the gospel and perform essential saving ordinances. They are charged with the same responsibility Jesus gave the original twelve apostles: "Go ye into all the world, and preach the gospel to every creature" (Mark 16:15). As they move forward in an effort to fulfill that commission, they will seek and receive more revelation from God. Undoubtedly, as circumstances change, so will policies, practices, levels of understanding, and application of principles change. And under the direction of the Almighty the work of the living church will steadily move forward, all as a part of bringing to pass the immortality and eternal life of man, which is the work and glory of God (see Moses 1:39).

We believe all that God has revealed, all that He does now reveal, and we believe that He will yet reveal many great and important things pertaining to the Kingdom of God.

9TH ARTICLE OF FAITH

HOW DO LATTER-DAY SAINTS BELIEVE THEY SHOULD LIVE THEIR LIVES?

"WE BELIEVE IN BEING HONEST, TRUE, CHASTE, BENEVOLENT, VIRTUOUS, AND in doing good to all men." Joseph Smith wrote this in 1842 in response to a journalist's inquiry concerning the beliefs of Latter-day Saints. "If there is anything virtuous, lovely, or of good report or praiseworthy, we seek after these things" (Articles of Faith 1:13). Latter-day Saints do not claim that they are all virtuous, without exception, nor that others do not display great virtue. Latter-day Saints do, however, feel strongly that their religious beliefs must be translated into daily living, and so they "seek after" those qualities of goodness.

AN OBLIGATION AND COVENANT

The charge to seek after virtue, goodness, honor, and all praiseworthy things is an obligation that flows from love for and devotion to God. Jesus declared, "Therefore all things whatsoever ye would that men should do to you, do ye even so to them: for this is the law and the prophets" (Matthew 7:12). Later in his ministry, Jesus further declared that loving God and loving our fellowmen are the two great commandments upon which "hang all the law and the prophets" (see Matthew 22:37–40). Latter-day Saints take

Photo by Craig Dimond. Courtesy of Welfare Department, Church of Jesus Christ of Latter-day Saints.

these commandments very seriously, for love is the essence of true religion (see James 1:27). "Though I speak with the tongues of men and of angels," the apostle Paul wrote, "and have not charity, I am become as sounding brass, or a tinkling cymbal. And though I have the gift of prophecy, and understand all mysteries, and all knowledge; and though I have all faith, so that I could remove mountains, and have not charity, I am nothing" (1 Corinthians 13:1–2; see Moroni 7:44–48). Latter-day Saints embrace the teachings of both ancient and modern scriptures that one's love for God must also be manifested in love for one's fellowmen.

People enter the Church of Jesus Christ of Latter-day Saints through baptism and take upon themselves a sacred covenant to love God with all their heart, might, mind, and strength and "serve him and keep his commandments" (Mosiah 18:10). They accept the obligation to try not only to keep the Lord's commandments, but also to become more like him—with hearts and lives more filled with purity, kindness, compassion, and mercy. Under this baptismal covenant, Latter-day Saints promise to show love for Christ by being "willing to bear one another's burdens, that they may be light," "to mourn with those that mourn; yea, and comfort those that stand in need of comfort" (Mosiah 18:8–9). It is this kind of concern for others and compassionate service that characterizes true discipleship (see John 13:34–35).

The extensive welfare system of the LDS Church and its humanitarian service throughout the world, as well as the acts of kindness and generosity exhibited by individual church members, are all byproducts of a sincere effort to love their fellowmen as the Savior admonished. This Christian service and compassion is not restricted to fellow believers or members of the LDS Church; it has no regard to race, religion, or nationality. "Respecting how much a man shall give annually," Joseph Smith declared, "we have no special instructions to give; he is to feed the hungry, to clothe the naked, to provide for the widow, to dry up the tear of the orphan, to comfort the afflicted, whether in this church or in any other, or in no church at all, wherever he finds them."[36]

RESULTS

Social scientists have observed that Latter-day Saints who devoutly espouse the teachings of their church, when compared to society in general, are:
- more likely to be happy in their marriages and satisfied with their family life and less likely to divorce.[37]
- less likely to engage in premarital or extramarital sexual behavior.[38]
- less likely to abuse drugs and alcohol.[39]

- more likely to enjoy strong mental health and experience less depression.[40]
- less likely to be involved in delinquent, deviant, or antisocial behaviors.[41]

Numerous other studies and many more sources could be cited to further highlight the positive nature of the Latter-day Saint way of life. The mountain of empirical evidence, however, can only describe; it cannot adequately explain why Latter-day Saints generally are happy, well-adjusted, and caring people. What, then, is the answer? "Little children, let no man deceive you," the apostle John wrote; "he that doeth righteousness is righteous, even as he is righteous" (1 John 3:7). The fruits of righteousness found in the lives of faithful Latter-day Saints come through striving to be true to their Christian covenants. While they faithfully and earnestly "seek after" those things that are "lovely, praiseworthy, or of good report," they recognize that these "fruits" come to them—blessing their own lives and enabling them to bless the lives of others—through the love and mercy of Jesus Christ.

Latter-day Saints believe that through the power of the Holy Spirit an individual who has accepted Christ through faith and obedience is "born again" and becomes a "new creature" in Christ (see 2 Corinthians 5:17; Ephesians 4:24–32; Mosiah 27:23–26). This spiritual transformation brings with it charity—the "pure love of Christ" (Moroni 7:47)—a love for Christ and also a love for others as Christ loves. The fruit of this spiritual rebirth includes goodness and righteousness, love, joy, peace, gentleness, and meekness (see Ephesians 5:9; Galatians 5:22–26). The newness of life that comes to one through the grace and mercy of Jesus Christ affects not only what one does outwardly but also what one is inwardly.

The Savior taught that things should be judged by their fruits (see Matthew 7:15–20). Prophets and churches should be judged by the product of their ministry and teachings. An individual's commitment to be a follower of Christ should be judged—if judged at all by mortals—by the quality of character and actions that commitment produces. Evil trees cannot bring forth good fruit, so good fruit is a sign of the goodness of the tree. Members of the restored Church of Jesus Christ believe that the fruits of the teachings of that church are obvious in their lives. They live their religion joyfully, peaceably, and with whole-souled devotion, seeking to pattern their lives after the perfect example of Jesus Christ. Their motivation for doing so comes from their love for the Lord and the sure testimony of the Spirit that burns in their hearts and inspires their minds. They are grateful beyond expression that the Savior accepts their commitment to him, forgives their transgressions, and blesses them with the good fruits of their devotion.

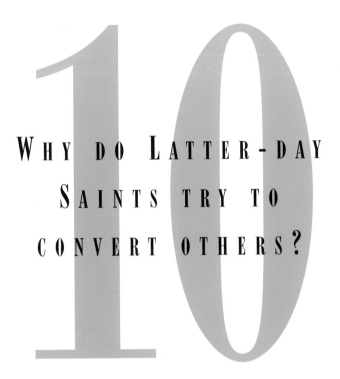

WHY DO LATTER-DAY SAINTS TRY TO CONVERT OTHERS?

MORMONS BELIEVE THAT THE CHURCH OF JESUS CHRIST OF LATTER-DAY Saints contains a *fulness* of the gospel of Jesus Christ and that this fulness is not found elsewhere. Therefore, they feel a responsibility to make the message of the restoration of Christ's Church available to all who will hear. They profess to have received the same commission from the Lord Jesus that he delivered to his followers anciently—to preach the gospel to people of all nations (see Matthew 28:19–20; Mark 16:15–18; see also D&C 68:8). This is the basis for the missionary system within the Church of Jesus Christ of Latter-day Saints.

One president of the LDS Church expressed these thoughts to those not of the LDS faith:

We have come not to take away from you the truth and virtue you possess. We have come not to find fault with you nor to criticize you. We have not come here to berate you because of things you have not done; but we have come here as your brethren. . . . and to say to you: "Keep all the good that you have, and let us bring to you more good,

in order that you may be happier and in order that you may be prepared to enter into the presence of our Heavenly Father."[42]

The Need

Latter-day Saints affirm that the answer to the world's problems—starvation, famine, disease, crime, inhumanity, and the dissolution of the family—is ultimately not found in social programs or legislation. Instead, the answer lies in the promise that God will change the hearts of those who have faith in Jesus Christ. There is much good being done by people of many Christian denominations to bring this message of Christ to a world that desperately needs it. Yet the Latter-day Saints declare that there is more truth to be known, more power to be exercised, and more profound fulfillment and joy to be found than is available in any other church. As one church leader pointed out, "We seek to bring all truth together. We seek to enlarge the circle of love and understanding among all the people

Latter-day Saints seek to follow the Savior's admonition to preach the gospel to all nations. [Painting by Harry Anderson, *Go Ye Therefore, and Teach All Nations*]

of the earth. Thus we strive to establish peace and happiness, not only within Christianity but among all mankind."[43]

THE MESSAGE

The restoration of the gospel came about as a divine response to the famine in the land foretold by Old Testament prophets—not a famine for bread nor a thirst for water, but a yearning to hear the word of God (see Amos 8:11–12). The fundamental message of Mormonism is:

- There is a God. He is our Father in Heaven.

- Jesus Christ is the divine Son of God and the promised Messiah. Salvation comes only in and through the redemption of Christ.

- Thus there is purpose to life. Our Heavenly Father has a plan for his children, a plan intended to bring peace and joy to all the sons and daughters of God through faith in Jesus Christ.

- God the Eternal Father and his Son Jesus Christ appeared to Joseph

Smith in the spring of 1820. This appearance began the restoration of the fulness of the gospel of Jesus Christ.

- Heavenly messengers have restored sacred truths and divine powers. Through those powers the church and kingdom of God have been reestablished on earth.

- God loves his children in this age and generation as much as he loved those to whom he sent his Son some two thousand years ago. The Father's perfect love is manifested not only in the preservation of the Bible, but also through modern revelation, modern scripture, modern apostles and prophets ordained with divine priesthood powers, and an inspired church organization.

THE CUSTODIAN

It is important to be a good person, a moral person, a person of integrity. Latter-day Saints believe, however, that the gospel is intended to do more than make us good persons. The gospel contains the power of God unto salvation (see Romans 1:16), the power to transform good people into Christlike people, noble souls into holy souls. The Church of Jesus Christ is the custodian of the gospel. Christ himself has given his restored church divine authority and the truths of salvation. So Latter-day Saints do not believe one can fully come unto Christ—and partake of all the blessings he offers—independent of (or in opposition to) the Church of Jesus Christ. They believe there is "one Lord, one faith, one baptism" (Ephesians 4:5) and that the sacraments or ordinances of salvation, administered by the priesthood held in his restored church, are prerequisite to entrance into the kingdom of God.

At a time in which there is a waning of belonging and in accordance with the scriptural command to share the gospel so that all might "come unto Christ, and be perfected in him" (Moroni 10:32), the Latter-day Saints invite all people to come home, to return to the family of God. The First Presidency of the LDS Church in 1907 declared, "Our motives are not selfish; our purposes not petty and earth-bound; we contemplate the human race, past, present and yet to come, as immortal beings, for whose salvation it is our mission to labor; and to this work, broad as eternity and deep as the love of God, we devote ourselves, now, and forever."[44]

THE
ARTICLES OF FAITH
OF THE CHURCH OF JESUS CHRIST
OF LATTER-DAY SAINTS

WE believe in God, the Eternal Father, and in His Son, Jesus Christ, and in the Holy Ghost.

2 We believe that men will be punished for their own sins, and not for Adam's transgression.

3 We believe that through the Atonement of Christ, all mankind may be saved, by obedience to the laws and ordinances of the Gospel.

4 We believe that the first principles and ordinances of the Gospel are: first, Faith in the Lord Jesus Christ; second, Repentance; third, Baptism by immersion for the remission of sins; fourth, Laying on of hands for the gift of the Holy Ghost.

5 We believe that a man must be called of God, by prophecy, and by the laying on of hands by those who are in authority, to preach the Gospel and administer in the ordinances thereof.

6 We believe in the same organization that existed in the Primitive Church, namely, apostles, prophets, pastors, teachers, evangelists, and so forth.

7 We believe in the gift of tongues, prophecy, revelation, visions, healing, interpretation of tongues, and so forth.

8 We believe the Bible to be the word of God as far as it is translated correctly; we also believe the Book of Mormon to be the word of God.

9 We believe all that God has revealed, all that He does now reveal, and we believe that He will yet reveal many great and important things pertaining to the Kingdom of God.

10 We believe in the literal gathering of Israel and in the restoration of the Ten Tribes; that Zion (the New Jerusalem) will be built upon the American continent; that Christ will reign personally upon the earth; and, that the earth will be renewed and receive its paradisiacal glory.

11 We claim the privilege of worshiping Almighty God according to the dictates of our own conscience, and allow all men the same privilege, let them worship how, where, or what they may.

12 We believe in being subject to kings, presidents, rulers, and magistrates, in obeying, honoring, and sustaining the law.

13 We believe in being honest, true, chaste, benevolent, virtuous, and in doing good to all men; indeed, we may say that we follow the admonition of Paul—We believe all things, we hope all things, we have endured many things, and hope to be able to endure all things. If there is anything virtuous, lovely, or of good report or praiseworthy, we seek after these things.

JOSEPH SMITH

1. *Teachings of the Prophet Joseph Smith*, sel. Joseph Fielding Smith (Salt Lake City: Deseret Book, 1976), 121.
2. C. S. Lewis, *Mere Christianity* (New York: Macmillan, 1952), 11.
3. Joseph Smith to John Wentworth, March 1842, in Joseph Smith Jr., *History of the Church of Jesus Christ of Latter-day Saints*, ed. B. H. Roberts, 7 vols. (Salt Lake City: Deseret Book, 1976), 4:536.
4. See Philip Schaff, *The Creeds of Christendom*, 3 vols. (Harper & Row, 1931; reprint, Grand Rapids, Mich.: Baker Books, 1985); and J. N. D. Kelly, *Early Christian Creeds*, 3rd ed. (New York: David McKay Co., 1972).
5. *Teachings of the Prophet Joseph Smith*, 56.
6. Ibid., 9–10.
7. *Improvement Era* 39 (November 1936): 660; see Victor L. Ludlow, "Bible," and Paul Hedengren, "Bible: LDS Beliefs in the Bible," in *Encyclopedia of Mormonism*, ed. Daniel H. Ludlow, 5 vols. (New York: Macmillan, 1992), 1:104–8.
8. *The Gospel Kingdom: Selections from the Writings and Discourses of John Taylor*, sel. G. Homer Durham (Salt Lake City: Bookcraft, 1987), 34.
9. See Joseph Smith, comp., *Lectures on Faith* (Salt Lake City: Deseret Book, 1985), 5:3; and *Teachings of the Prophet Joseph Smith*, 346–48.
10. President Snow often referred to this couplet as having been revealed to him by inspiration during the Nauvoo period of the church. See, for example, *Deseret Weekly,* 3 November 1894, 610; *Deseret Weekly,* 8 October 1898, 513; *Deseret News,* 15 June 1901, 177; and Journal History of the Church, Historical Department, Church of Jesus Christ of Latter-day Saints, Salt Lake City, 20 July 1901, 4.
11. Irenaeus, *Against Heresies*, bk. 5, preface.
12. Ibid., 4.38 (4); compare 4.11 (2): "But man receives progression and increase towards God. For as God is always the same, so also man, when found in God, shall always progress towards God."
13. Clement of Alexandria, *Exhortation to the Greeks*, 1.
14. Clement of Alexandria, *The Instructor*, 3.1. See his *Stromateis*, 23.
15. Justin Martyr, *Dialogue with Trypho*, 124.
16. Athanasius, *Against the Aryans*, 1.39, 3.34.
17. Athanasius, *On the Incarnation*, 54.
18. Augustine, *On the Psalms*, 50.2. Augustine insists that such individuals are gods by grace rather than by nature, but they are gods nevertheless.
19. Richard P. McBrien, *Catholicism*, 2 vols. (Minneapolis: Winston Press, 1980), 1:146, 156, emphasis in original.
20. Symeon Lash, "Deification," in *The Westminster Dictionary of Christian Theology*, ed. Alan Richardson and John Bowden (Philadelphia: Westminster Press, 1983), 147–48.
21. C. S. Lewis, *The Weight of Glory and Other Addresses*, rev. ed. (New York: Macmillan, Collier Books, 1980), 18.
22. Lewis, *Mere Christianity*, 174–75. For a more recent example of the doctrine of deification in modern, non-LDS Christianity, see M. Scott Peck, *The Road Less Traveled* (New York: Simon and Schuster, 1978), 269–70: "For no matter how much we may like to pussyfoot around it, all of us who postulate a loving God and really think about it eventually come to a single terrifying idea: God wants us to become Himself (or Herself or Itself). We are growing toward godhood."
23. Smith, *History of the Church*, 6:305.
24. *The Teachings of Lorenzo Snow*, comp. Clyde J. Williams (Salt Lake City: Bookcraft, 1984), 2.
25. Smith, *History of the Church,* 6:306–7.
26. Joseph Fielding Smith, *Doctrines of Salvation*, comp. Bruce R. McConkie, 3 vols. (Salt Lake City: Bookcraft, 1954–56), 1:12; see Bruce R. McConkie, *The Promised Messiah* (Salt Lake City: Deseret Book, 1978), 166.
27. In *Journal of Discourses*, 26 vols. (Liverpool: F. D. Richards & Sons, 1851–86), 11:249; see 7:333.
28. In ibid., 4:271; see Joseph F. Smith, *Gospel Doctrine* (Salt Lake City: Deseret Book, 1978), 64.
29. Smith, *History of the Church,* 6:303; see Brigham Young, in *Journal of Discourses,* 13:312.
30. Lewis, *Mere Christianity*, 129.

31. Bruce R. McConkie, *Doctrinal New Testament Commentary*, 3 vols. (Salt Lake City: Bookcraft, 1965–73), 2:499, 500.
32. In Conference Report, October 1988, 78.
33. *Teachings of the Prophet Joseph Smith*, 301; see 297, 305.
34. David O. Mckay, *Gospel Ideals* (Salt Lake City: Improvement Era, 1953), 6, emphasis in original; see Brigham Young, in *Journal of Discourses,* 1:131; 8:124–25.
35. *Teachings of the Prophet Joseph Smith*, 256–57.
36. *Times and Seasons* 3 (15 March 1842): 732.
37. See Melvin L. Wilkinson and William C. Tanner III, "The Influence of Family Size, Interaction, and Religiosity on Family Affection in a Mormon Sample," *Journal of Marriage and the Family* 42/2 (1980): 297–304.
38. See Brent C. Miller and Terrance D. Olson, "Sexual Attitudes and Behavior of High School Students in Relation to Background and Contextual Factors," *Journal of Sex Research* 24 (1988): 194–200.
39. See Ricky D. Hawks and Steven J. Bahr, "Religion and Drug Use," *Journal of Drug Education* 22/1 (1992): 1–8.
40. See Allen E. Bergin et al., "Religion and Mental Health: Mormons and Other Groups," in *Contemporary Mormonism: Social Science Perspectives*, ed. Marie Cornwall, Tim B. Heaton, and Lawrence A. Young (Urbana: University of Illinois Press, 1994), 138–58.
41. See Bruce A. Chadwick and Brent L. Top, "Religiosity and Delinquence among LDS Adolescents," *Journal for the Scientific Study of Religion* 32/1 (1993): 51–67.
42. George Albert Smith, *Sharing the Gospel with Others*, comp. Preston Nibley (Salt Lake City: Deseret Book, 1948), 12, 13.
43. Howard W. Hunter, *That We Might Have Joy* (Salt Lake City: Deseret Book, 1994), 59.
44. Cited in ibid.

Illustration Credits

Come unto me, all ye that labour and are heavy laden, and I will give you rest. MATTHEW 11:28

Come unto Christ, and be perfected in him. MORONI 10:32
[*The Christus* replica by Aldo Rebechi from the original by Bertel Thorvaldsen]